Barbed Wire and Roses

Gothic Chamber Tales

Andrea Dean Van Scoyoc

ISBN - 978-81-19654-62-8
Cyberwit.net

ALL artwork within this book (including the cover) is AI-assisted by word prompt and is not eligible for, nor can be considered copyright material in any way.

All stories and poetry within this collection are based on pure fiction and are a creative figment of the author's dark imagination.

Any semblance to actual persons, places or things is 100% pure coincidence and must be treated as such.

~Foreword:~

The imagination is a strange and mysterious thing.

It can take you to places of beauty in dreams from a wish from which you never want to wake...to nightmares of such darkness and heart wrenching pain, that you wake up with a racing heart, sometimes even in tears grateful to leave that horrific realm behind.

It is between both of these worlds that I dwell...somewhere in shadowed light...somewhere just outside the light...somewhere in dusk's embrace.

Within the pages of this book, I hope to introduce you to this world...**my** world.

It's not for everyone, but for those who can weather the journey, I think you'll find that it's a one-of-a-kind trip.

In Darkness...

Andrea Dean Van Scoyoc

Chapter One

Sea Spray Song

Lightning flashed all around her, treating her almost as if she were a magnet for Zeus's anger. As she stood on the edge of the cliff, her long Gothic dress billowing out behind her in the howling wind, her eyes were fixed on the crashing surf below, the cool salt spray assailing her nostrils and...had she been closer, stinging her cheeks. No matter, she could imagine the feel of the wet assault and she closed her eyes, willing herself to another time...another place...

The power of the waves were hypnotic. She could feel them as they called to her, luring her to the icy world below, the ground trembling as the white foam crashed against the rocks. The wind whipped her hair around her face almost as a veil to hide from her what she desired most but she felt the energy of the waves rushing through her veins.

She was lost in the ethereal dream of it all, feeling the might of the ocean and transfixed by the beauty of the moment.

She absorbed the strength of the sea, the immenseness of the waves and the wildness of nature. She was held…as if by some phantom power; the surge of the tide and the sound of the wind in her ears; the titanic ocean rushing through her.

She felt both alive…*and* at peace, connected to the feral beauty of the ocean kingdom, this magical world of wet wonder, a realm she'd only dreamed of within the confines of her small world.
But…here…now she would call to the element of her yearning, her true nature…the unchained and longing depths of the crushing underwater mansions that she knew awaited her.
They would be hers…

Chapter Two

Roses On Gravestones

There she stood, an undead beauty, a vampire of eternal life...eternal thirst, but always yearning for the delicacy she knew life still held.

She'd never forgotten her favorite place...even before she was turned...the cemetery.
Beautiful, dangerous and yet alluring, she stood, as she had so many times before in this...her forever home.

Home. That word held new meaning for her now as, before, the word had been just that...a word.
It was a dream, a passing fancy...a whim. She'd joked so many times about how she would love to live in a cemetery and now...

Her wish had come true.
Not exactly the way she desired, but no matter.

It was the Witching Hour... *her* hour as her eyes lazily scanned the tombstones.
The night mist that lingered, cloaking her in chill...a chill she *wished* she could feel had been her companion since she'd ventured forth from the rotting depths of the cool undercroft she'd made her very own.

What she *could* feel were the presence of the ghosts that surrounded her and so her thoughts drifted to the stories she had heard about them.
She wondered if they were here to protect her or if they had come to take her away to the afterlife.
She had no fear of them, as she knew she would never die, but she couldn't help but be intrigued by their presence, wondering if they knew that they too...could never be whole again?
She now felt a strong connection to this potter's field and the spirits that haunted it.

Before she joined the world of the lost, the forgotten and the damned; while this place had always been a comfort to her, never could she have dreamed that it would be hers in which to dwell.
There was a strange satisfaction in knowing that she wasn't alone.
As she stood there, she thought of all the stories she had heard, growing up, about this tract of ancient, local lore and the creatures that lurked within.

She was one of those creatures now, the moss and moldy walls of her darkened chamber; hers to never leave if she so wished.
How strange that an entity...one so accursed as she now was, could feel at home on holy ground...if this place could even still be considered holy. Long left to the ravages of use and neglect, no prayers were whispered here any longer...no hymns sung.
But one thing was certain...she could sense the energy whipping the trees and howling in

otherworldly cries that remained here as if transfixed by some supernatural host.

Whether for benevolence or malevolence she could not say, nor did she care, but she did wonder if she could use it to help her in her search for answers.

She closed her eyes and let the power of this resting place place wash over her, allowing her to access a deeper level of understanding that she had never known before.

Eternity afforded her all the time she needed and with this newfound understanding, she felt empowered by a force she'd never had in life.
Answers, everything she'd ever craved...it could now be hers.
"Patience darling...patience," the spirits whispered.

Chapter Three

Tales Through Time

One of the spookiest tales that has been told in our small town is of a ghostly woman singing in our park's gazebo.

On some nights, she appears in the center of the park and then walks to the gazebo. Others, she simply materializes in the ornate little shelter surrounded by a dense fog.

The more romantically inclined women of the town will breathe that her song is so beautiful and haunting it can bring even the strongest of men to tears.

No one knows if she is a spirit, a fanciful play of light and shape, or a cunning and stealthy woman of flesh and blood, desperate to share her talent, who crafts the story that follows her for an elaborate promotional campaign.

Those who are fully vested in the spirit legend, relay the story that she was once a young woman of wealth and means from a prominent family, who fell in love with a man of common class.
She was forced to give him up and eventually died of a broken heart.
From then on, for as long as the story has endured, she has appeared in the gazebo, singing *her* song.
Those who *claim* to have seen her, repeat this tale with wide eyed endearment, as if they knew her before her demise. Still others repeat the tale wistfully…as if quoting from a bygone fairytale.
Whether or not this tale is one of flights of fancy and overactive imagination or whether it is based on some semblance of fact, the only real truth remains that…

Everyone in the town, at some point or another...has **heard** the song.

Chapter Four
Them

On a clear night at every full moon, a beautiful ghost couple can be seen wandering through a secluded forest on the outskirts of a local town.

They make their way through the thick foliage, their ethereal figures illuminated by the moonlight. As they pass by, a light breeze carries the sweet scent of flowers and the rustling of leaves that seem to whisper their secrets into the night.

The couple's faces are expressionless, but their eyes are full of sorrow and longing for something out of reach.

As they move deeper into the forest, the trees seem to bow in reverence at their presence. They move slowly, quietly, as if trying to keep their secrets hidden from the world. Even the animals of the night are in awe of the beautiful couple, stopping to watch them as they almost silently glide by.

Eventually the couple reaches a clearing and stops, standing still in the bright light of the moon. It is here that they whisper their secrets to the night, their words lost on the breeze as they fade into the darkness.

Who they are, no one knows. Many theories have been postulated, but none are aggressively pursued as... like some secrets...like some *things*...they are left better off alone.

Chapter Five

The Night The Roses Came For Me

(Told in first person as I experienced it)

As I stood at the cemetery gate, the smell of roses filled the air, and I couldn't help but feel a chill run down my spine.

I could see the silhouette of a figure in the darkness, standing still and silent, with an eerie presence that seemed to linger. I was sure it was a ghost, watching me from the shadows. I felt the hairs on the back of my neck stand on end as I watched it, unable to move or speak.

I felt a deep sense of dread, but also a strange sense of security. It was an odd recognition of being totally helpless whether within the walls of the burial grounds, or on the outside.

The ghost's presence was calming and comforting, despite the fear I felt and that feeling, that feeling of being captured by that heady scent of romance truly engulfed me to the point of losing all senses as I breathed in the smell of the abundant roses.

The cemetery was silent and peaceful, and I closed my eyes...but I could sense that the ghost was still there.

I remained, clutching the gate, half in terror, half in the aid I needed in standing because I truly feared opening my eyes. Would *it* be before me? Would it have slid in beside me?

Eventually, I could stay my fate no longer and I slowly, achingly slitted my eyes.

The figure in the darkness slowly faded away, but the scent of the roses remained.

It began to rain...

Chapter Six
The Gatekeeper's Visit

The woman stood in a Gothic manor, her eyes fixed on the ornate stained glass window, captivated by the intricate details of the antique, faded colors throwing their hue on the worn and splintered hardwood floor.

The bright colors of the aged pieces blended together to form a beautiful masterpiece and even in the chill, the scant light streaming through the window cast her face in a warm glow.

It was the grand staircase, however, that mesmerized her and cemented in her mind the grandeur of the manor. She could almost feel the presence of the generations that came before her and the stories they had to tell.

Her breath caught as she took in the features of the room, the high ceilings, the ornate furnishings, the thick walls that stood the test of time.

Rapt admiration and respect for the craftsmanship of the window, for the skill that went into creating it...the entire house, every nook, every cranny, filled her.
She could only imagine the time and effort that went into this once splendid home and the love of every detail as it was shaped, smoothed and perfected by hand.
Her breath in her throat, she took it all in and felt connected to people she'd never met, people she could never know and a time she wished she could have enjoyed.

Chapter Seven
Time To Let Go

The graveyard was eerie and desolate, with its aging headstones and statues coated in a thick layer of dust. The trees were dead and leafless, their branches twisted and gnarled like the fingers of skeletal hands reaching up from beneath the earth.
The only sound was the wind whistling through the branches, creating a chill that ran down his spine. He was gripped by a strange sense of foreboding as he stepped closer inside the rusted gate hanging precariously from its stone foundation.

His heart pounded as he valiantly attempted to ignore the wild throbbing in his temples. He was being watched...he was certain of it. The presence of the dead who lay beneath the ground, their spirits lingering in the air wanted him...he was certain of it.

Despite its beauty, there was something undeniably creepy about this abandoned haunted cemetery and while he had been drawn to it, he did not want to stay.

Chapter Eight
Solo Sojourn

It was a quiet, moonless night, and the woman was alone in the woods. She held a lantern in one hand, its light a beacon in the darkness. As she walked, she felt the cool night air brushing against her skin, and heard the sound of night creatures rustling in the underbrush.

The trees loomed overhead, their branches casting strange shadows in the pale light. A faint mist had settled over the woods, adding to the feeling of mystery and awe.

She continued on, feeling a strange sense of belonging; she wasn't certain as to what, but she felt as if she were not intruding and that, instead, she'd been expected!

With no idea where she was going, she had the feeling that she was being guided by an unseen force, deeper into the forest. Her steps were slow and steady, her only companion the gentle glow of her lantern and the soft whisper of the wind.

Time seemed to pass slowly, and the woman felt at one with the world around her, enveloped by the energy of the trees, of the earth and of the moonless sky. She felt like she was in a dream, and nothing mattered except for the moment.

A clearing loomed before her and briefly she felt a twinge of fear. But she quickly realized there was nothing to be afraid of, and the clearing seemed to welcome her, much like the rest of the forest had. She rested her lantern on the ground and looked up at the stars, feeling a profound sense of connection to the universe around her.

She knew she'd never find her way back home, but she also knew that she didn't need to. She felt that she was exactly where she was meant to be, in the middle of the woods, another world to her, another time...another place.

All was well and she'd be fine...just she and her comforting lantern.

Chapter Nine
Old Wounds

The potter's field sat on the outskirts of town, its once lush green fields now overgrown with weeds and wildflowers. The sun beat down on the neglected graves, casting eerie shadows on the cracked and weathered tombstones. It was a place that was often avoided by the living, for it held a dark and haunted past.

Her Granny had told her the story many times as a child. Until she ventured to the wretched soil herself, she had not been entirely certain it was real.

Many years ago, the land was used as a burial ground for those who couldn't afford a proper funeral or were simply forgotten by their loved ones. The graves were dug deep and the bodies were laid to rest without any markers or headstones. No one cared for these souls who were left bereft and cold in the rutted and discarded field.

As time went by, the potter's field became more and more of an eye sore. No one cared, no one was left to care. The ground was as forgotten as the hapless spirits entombed there.

The once bustling town had grown and expanded, leaving the field and the poorest of its earliest inhabitants, behind. The graves were now hidden beneath layers of dirt and debris, making it nearly impossible to distinguish one from another. The only reminder of the lives that were lost were the scattered and broken pieces of pottery left behind.

The pasture, for that is all it had become, giving way to a melancholic aura, as if the shades of the forgotten still roamed the grounds, longing for someone to remember them. The wind whistled through the tall grass, as if whispering the stories of those who were laid to rest there...back when they had families, back when they had smiles, hope and life...to share.

Some have said that on quiet nights, with a keen ear, faint cries and the moans of the restless, trapped in this abandoned place, pierce the night, screaming for the release they never fully received.

Despite its eerie reputation, some brave and curious folk have ventured into the potter's field to tiptoe through the overgrown paths, careful not to disturb the final resting place of the forgotten. Some have left flowers or trinkets on the graves, a small gesture to show that those weary and worn shadows left there... have not been completely forgotten.

But as with all good intentions, as time passed, the visits became scarcer and scarcer until the land was, again, no more than a forlorn and withered patch left to decay and be reclaimed by nature. The memories of those who were buried there slowly faded, their stories lost to time until only a few remembered what the land was even used for.

And yet, even in its disgraceful state, the potter's field has always held a certain beauty. The sunset behind the tombstones cast a golden glow over the town, as a halo of protection almost...as if the inhabitants say, "You may have forgotten us, but we continue to look after you."

The wildflowers still bloom, adding splashes of color to the otherwise dull landscape and with the moonrise each evening, the wretched and disgraced land comes alive with the whispers of the forgotten, reminding us that even in death, they have each other and us, even, though we don't appreciate them...so they are truly never alone.

Chapter Ten
Winds of Change

The beautiful but distraught woman wandered the beach during the storm, her long dress cascading in flowing undulations in the wind behind her.

The waves crashed against the shore, and the smell of the bitter night air filled her lungs with each breath. She felt the raindrops on her skin, and the thunder echoed in the night sky. Despite the storm, she was captivated by the beauty of the beach. The moonlight glittered off the waves, and the sand was cool beneath her feet.

She walked along the shore, marveling at how something so soothing in one moment, could be so angry in the next. As she walked further, the crackles of lightning shattered the ebon sky like fiery swords slicing through black velvet.

She stopped to watch the electric fingers, captivated by their grace and beauty. The storm picked up as the sky let loose a torrent of ice cold rain and as it raged around her, it only bolstered her desire to stay.

She walked, screaming into the night…a primal cry of all her anguish, all her frustrations…all her dreams that never came true until the storm had passed, and the beach was solemn in peaceful silence.

She was left with a deep appreciation for the power of nature, and the awesome strength the beach had revealed to her, allowing her to share in it… with it that night.

Chapter Eleven
Secrets

The old, antique mirror hung on the wall of the abandoned mansion, its ornate frame weathered and chipped with age. As the moonlight poured through the dusty windows, the mirror seemed to come to life, its surface rippling and shimmering as if it held a secret within.

And indeed, it did.

For, within the mirror, there lived a beautiful ghost, haunting its reflective surface, for centuries.

Her name was Isadora, and she had been trapped within the mirror by a powerful curse placed upon her by a jealous lover.

Isadora's ghostly form was as ethereal and captivating as she herself had been in life. Eyes of pure ebon and hair as wild and dark as an angry sky, her long white dress flowing around her like a cloud.

Those black eyes glowed out through the mirror with a hatred that not even the depths of time could tame.

Though trapped within the mirror, unable to leave its confines, she was not alone, for she could see into the mortal world and her hatred of those who got to live, while she was imprisoned, grew.

She had been trapped within the mirror for so long she had lost track of time.

She watched as the mansion fell into ruin, as the once grand halls were covered in cobwebs and dust. She had seen generations of owners come and go, but none had ever been able to break the curse and release her from her prison...and a few brave of heart and stalwart of spirit had indeed tried.

But one night, as the moon was full and the stars were bright, a young woman entered the mansion. Her name was Lili, and she had been drawn to the abandoned mansion by...she wasn't sure, but she knew she had to get inside, for something ...some*one*...was awaiting her.

As she explored the dark and eerie rooms, she came upon the old mirror and knew that this...this one decrepit object was her goal. And as she gazed into its depths, she saw a faint figure standing behind her own reflection.

Isadora had never been able to make complete contact with anyone who looked into the mirror, no matter how hard she tried.

She had only been able to direct those who'd tried to help her, to her tattered and fragile diary, hidden in the desk drawer under her prison.

But there was something different about Lili. She could sense a kindred spirit within the young woman, and she reached out to her, trying to communicate and managed to point to the drawer and the sad story of her entrapment. At first, Lili was afraid, but as she read Isadora's story and learned about the curse that bound her, she felt a deep sense of compassion and a desire to help.

Together, Isadora and Lili worked to break the curse and release the beautiful spirit from her prison. It was a difficult and dangerous journey, but with each passing day, they grew closer, forming a bond that transcended the physical world.
Each day, Lili would visit and each day, she would get closer to releasing the hopeful discarnate and finally, on the night of the next full moon, they succeeded. Isadora was freed from the mirror, her beautiful ghostly form now able to roam the physical world once again.

From that day on, Isadora and Lili were inseparable. Isadora was once again, home but more importantly, she had found a friend and a kindred spirit in Lili. And as for the mirror, it remained on the wall, a reminder of the curse that had once bound Isadora, but also a symbol of the newfound friendship and the beautiful ghost that had once haunted its surface.

Chapter Twelve
Sweet Morning

As the early morning mist rolled in across the desolate countryside, a figure clad in a long, black dress emerged from the fog. She moved slowly across the damp grass, her bare feet not making a sound as her dress trailed behind her.
Enveloped in an aura of mystery and darkness, her long black hair cascaded down her back in waves. She seemed to be searching for something, her eyes darting around the landscape for a sign.
As she walked, the bottom of her dress heavy with dew, she continued her search in the cool, dawn air.

The sun began to peek out from behind the clouds, illuminating the shroud that cloaked everything.
Her dark clothing a stark contrast to the bright morning light, she seemed unbothered by the chill in the air, her steps still strong and purposeful. The sun began to warm the countryside, and the woman moved onward, never wavering in her search, the only sound

the crunch of her footsteps on the wet grass.
Still, she did not hurry, her head held high as she walked through the mist. As the sun rose higher in the sky, the woman disappeared into the waning mist, the only evidence of her having been there at all...her small footsteps left in the dew and the smell of her perfume on the air.

Chapter Thirteen
Weep No More

She stood in front of the tomb, her funeral shroud joyfully dancing in the wind as if not understanding its duty.
Her dark hair trickled down her shoulders in tangled waves, mimicking the turmoil in her heart. Tears streamed down her pale cheeks, glistening in the moonlight as she wept for the loss of her beloved. She clutched a wilted bouquet of dark red roses, their thorns pricking her skin, a painful reminder of the sharp edges of grief as her blood ran as heavily as her tears.

The tomb before her was adorned with intricate carvings of angels and demons, a symbol of the eternal struggle between life and death and her eyes were drawn to the name etched in stone - her lover's name. It felt like a stab to her heart, a cruel reminder that he was gone forever.

Memories flooded her mind, of happier times spent with her love. The laughter, the embraces, the passionate kisses - all now just distant pictures in her mind. She couldn't imagine a world without him by her side, and yet here she was, standing alone at his final resting place.

She sank to her knees and whispered his name, the weight of her sorrow too heavy to bear as she traced her fingers over the cold stone.
Oh if only it could bring her some comfort, some sense of connection to her lost love. But all she felt was emptiness, a void that could never be filled.

The night was silent, save for the woman's sobs and the rustling of leaves in the wind. The moon's pale light cast an eerie glow over the scene, adding to the hallowed and horrific heartache of the moment. It was as if the universe itself was mourning the loss of their love.

As the woman wept, she couldn't help but wonder if she would ever find happiness again. A part of her died with her lover, and she couldn't imagine ever being whole again. But as she gazed at the tomb, she made a promise to keep his memory alive, to honor his life and the love they shared.

With the first rays of the sun, she stood up, her tear-stained face a picture of quiet strength and placed the roses on the tomb, a final tribute to her love. As she turned to walk away, she knew that she would carry his memory with her, always and forever.
As she vowed to love him in life, that resolve would not waiver in death.

Chapter Fourteen
Missed Opportunities

There's never a morn that comes,
That isn't fraught with tears,
An imagined world of love and light
No worry, evil or fears.

Live each day to its best
But remember we all must die,
The clock is ticking so try to smile,
There is no time to cry...

Do we share our path with many,
Or do we share with few?
Do we share our thoughts and dreams,
And all that we can do?
Or are we secretive and walk alone
To let our secrets lie,
Never knowing that on any given day,
All we know will die?
What do we say to one another when we pass along the street?
Do we nod in acquiescence or do we stop to meet?

In each person we see, and all that we do and say,
Each and every living soul is simply a walking corpse that day.

There is no rule of thumb for living your life at all,
Live it well, live it poorly, because in the end we'll fall
Do we decay to age, or to disease or to the ravages of pain?
All we can be assured of is when that final time does come...
We'll never be whole again...

The morning cries, "Let me in, I want to stay,"
The dusk cries, "Let me in, Time to die this day,"
We live for dawn and die to dusk,
Decayed by life's long journey and pain,
When we're ready to go,

Is there happiness at wayfares finally
closed long last
Or are we happy to never see those we
loathe ever again?
Life is filled with those we love and those we
equally despise,
Death is a release from all the challenges
we've failed,
And all the triumphs we threw aside.

Chapter Fifteen
Rage

The wind howled fiercely, whipping through the barren trees and sending leaves and branches flying in all directions. The rain pelted down, creating a symphony of drumming on the frayed rooftops and shattered windows.

But amidst the chaos of the storm, there were other sounds that could be heard; mournful cries and whispers seemed to ride on the gusts of wind, echoing through the deserted streets and desolate buildings.

It was as if the storm itself was alive, crying out in pain and despair at something only it could suffer.

Huddled in what buildings could offer them at least some shelter, those that weren't too afraid to speculate, spoke of spirits of the restless dead, trapped in the violent winds and raging waters. Others believed it was the wails of the damned, imploring for one last chance. As the storm raged on, the cries and whispers grew louder and more desperate, filling the air with a haunting and eerie reminder of the forces of nature and the unknown mysteries that lurked in the shadows. And as the storm eventually passed, leaving behind a trail of further destruction and chaos on the already beleaguered town, the mournful cries and whispers faded away, leaving only a lingering sense of unease and wonder in its wake.

Chapter Sixteen
The End

In eternity's sorrow, there's nothing to do but weep,
Only in memory doth the living keep,
A somber dance where shadows gently rest,
"Time will make it better," some suggest,
But as the clock ticks away, time passes with its fleeting face,
In forever slumber an empty aching space...

In the hush of night, whispers softly sigh,
Souls depart this life forevermore
And there's nothing to do but cry,

Memories linger, like echoes in the dark,
Haunting the living, dousing all sparks
For eternity's sorrow is a timeless ache,
A heart's lament, a soul's burning hate,

But in the depths of grief, a way to cope,
A shard of light, a glimpse of hope,

Death claims us all and while tears will fall,
Memory remains... lingering in us all,
In our darkest moments we find shadow's
grace,
One final, "I love you," before death's cold
embrace,
Solace in pain,
Remembrance in rain,
Strength for the journey
Support for the way
Lingering spirits holding onto eternity's
thread,
Only unraveling into nothingness after were
dead...

~Author Bio: ~

A rat's nest for hair and fire in her eyes ...
She needs no one...because no one has ever needed her...
Like a wild vine she climbs toward the light...but shrinks from its burning heat
The night calls her, for it knows her by name
Whispers in the darkness...dark souls awaiting her company

~Official Website: ~

https://linktr.ee/theandreadeanvanscoyoc

www.ingramcontent.com/pod-product-compliance
Lightning Source LLC
LaVergne TN
LVHW091221150826
845673LV00014B/1121

* 9 7 8 8 1 1 9 6 5 4 6 2 8 *